DROPSHIPPING GOLDMINE: LAUNCH A PROFITABLE DROPSHIPPING BUSINESS WITH THIS SIMPLE PROVEN STRATEGY

DAVID NELSON

Want to know how to scale your Shopify store or any business to $1k per day with Facebook advertisement? Click the link below to be the first person to know when I launch my next book on Advance Facebook Marketing Strategy

http://marketinglikepro.launchrock.com/

Copyright © 2018 by David Nelson. All Right Reserved.

No part of this publication may be reproduced, distributed, or transmitted in any form or by any means, including photocopying, recording, or other electronic or mechanical methods, or by any information storage and retrieval system without the prior written permission of the publisher, except in the case of very brief quotations embodied in critical reviews and certain other noncommercial uses permitted by copyright law.

Thank you for buying

Dropshipping Goldmine: Launch a Profitable Dropshipping Business with This Simple Proven Strategy

Table of Contents

Why I Wrote This

Why You Should Read This Book

Chapter 1. Why Shopify is the Best Ecommerce Platform

Chapter 2. How To Create Shopify Store

Chapter 3. Niche And Product Research Strategy

Chapter 4. Best Platform To Find Supplier

Chapter 5. Best Apps For Importing Product

Chapter 6. Other App To Increase Sale

Chapter 7. How To Write Title And Description And Product pricing

Chapter 8. Marketing Intro

Chapter 9. Influencer Marketing

Chapter 10. Facebook Marketing

Chapter 11. Quora Marketing

Chapter 12. Reddit Marketing

About The Author

Other Books By David Nelson

Connect With Me

WHY I WROTE THIS

After seeing a lot of people struggling with their dropshipping business. I decided to lay out a complete guide, trick and strategy to create, run and own a profitable Shopify dropshipping business in less than one month.

Again have spent a lot of time on Reddit and Quora in answering question base on dropshipping and the major question I see most beginner and intermediate dropshipper asking like; is Shopify dropshipping dead, is dropshipping still profitable and why am I getting traffic (I personally review their store) but no sale?

The answer to the first two question above is yes. Shopify dropshipping or dropshipping on any platform is profitable but the major problem most people face is either of too many information (jumping from one mentor to another, watching tons of video on youtube, reading from different blog post) and having little or no budget for testing the product.

The second question is because their store description sucks e.g. there is no scarcity, urgency and product story: **why will people buy sunglass from you if you don't tell them the danger behind exposing their eye to the sun.** Get the idea?

Again they don't know how to optimize their store for more conversion e.g. no upsell and no similar product to display for the customer to buy more product and the traffic most of them drive to there store is not a target (quality) traffic.

You will learn how to avoid all the mistake and do this in a perfect way.

After struggling for 4 years before earning a cent with my e-commerce store, I decided to share the same method that has really work for me in this book.

I know a lot of people are also in the same shoe as I was 4 years back when I was cracking the code to e-commerce secret, today you don't have to spend the same time I spent learning from different ecom mentor because this book outlines all that have learnt so far and you will discover what works best in the ecom world.

if you can follow step by step guide outline in this book, you can create a profitable online store in less than a few months from now that generate consistent 5 to 6 figure even if you have no experience.

Why You Should Read This Book

The strategy I outline in this book will help you grow your own brand (online store) fast.

If you are serious about starting a business, go on vacation with your family and work at home in your own space then you have to read this book to the fullness.

After reading this book and implement everything you learn, I believe you will be able to stop your 9 to 5 job and take this as a full-time job.

You don't need to own an inventory for this type of business. Every product you sell will be dropship to your customer by your supplier.

If you implement what I teach in this book, you will be able to make over $10,000 and earn five to six figures monthly

This book takes you from ordinary beginner to being an expert in the next few days

Note: You will not make your first $1000 to $10k if you don't put the system outlined in this book into action.

And most importantly, if you are looking to get rich quick this book is not for you and you will be disappointed but if you put everything learnt into action you are on your way to own a profitable dropshipping business that will deposit money to your bank regularly and even make you a million dollar plus in the next few years.

To your success,

David Nelson

Chapter 1. Why Shopify is the Best E-commerce Platform

If you have ever thought of starting an e-commerce business and worried about the platform to go with then I will suggest reading the entire book to know the right platform for you

Again have you try different platform like installing woocommerce themes on your WordPress site and thinking whether to start or switch to Shopify?

Keep reading to discover what to do next

At the end of this chapter, you will discover why Shopify is the best e-commerce platform to start your e-commerce business

Also, you will discover why to focus on creating your own brand and not to waste your time affiliating with big e-commerce sites like Amazon, eBay, Banggood and Etsy though it's also a good one to go with.

Before we dive into this, let discourse little about woocommerce and other big brands like Amazon, eBay, banggoog and Etsy

Woocommerce is a WordPress e-commerce theme designed for people who are interested in running an e-commerce business. When designing woocommerce you need to work on a lot of technical stuff like designing the buy now button, tackling the payment method, adding product manually, no sale pop up plugins like Shopify, very hard to work with some china and united state print on demand company like teelaunch, pillow profit and so on.

Time will not permit me to discourse or cover some other feature woocommerce lack. You can make research on that.

There are also some e-commerce companies like eBay, banggood, Amazon and Etsy that most people affiliate with and start promoting there product.

You are missing a lot of meat and potato doing these!!

Working with the listed company above isn't bad at all but it kills your business and stops you from making more money in your e-commerce carrier

Though you can still affiliate with this company but let it be a side project while focusing on creating your own brand with Shopify

These companies started one day by someone and grow to where they are today

You can also be that next person that will build the next big (brand) and most trusted e-commerce business.

THE REASON NOT TO START E-COMMERCE BUSINESS WITH AMAZON, EBAY, BANGGOOD AND ETSY

Like I said above that you are missing and losing a lot of meat and potato if your e-commerce business depends on this big company above

Here is the reason

I want you to know that the key to success in any online business is DATA! And these so-called big company above keep their data to themselves and never share it with anyone

Despite sending traffic through paid advert to these companies, they still intend to keep the data to themselves and hide it from you.

This is where every e-commerce entrepreneur needs to think smarter and need to start creating their own brand through Shopify platform

Think of sending those traffic to your Shopify store

Consider this

You can re-market and re-target this audience through several ways like

- facebook marketing strategy using custom and lookalike audience and optimize for purchase

- you got their email when they order your product so you can promote similar product to them every week base on their interest. The list is endless

I believe you are thinking smarter now

Do this math

Think of having 10,000 or more (anyone who purchases your product automatically subscribes to your store email list) email subscriber on your Shopify store! What did you think that will be with a product that earns you $10, $20 even $2 or above in revenue

That is more money to your bottom line!! Not to talk of ADD TO CART or ABANDONED CART that can be retargeted through Facebook marketing.

Research and experience make us understand that 90% of people directed to your store through advert do not purchase any product from you but with access to DATA we can retarget and remarket to them through facebook marketing or retarget them through google ads which also will lead to more success.

I believe we have discussed some of the benefits of Shopify above but let dive more deeply into Shopify platform below

Before that

I believe that we already know little about woocommerce and also the reason not to start an e-commerce business with a big e-commerce company like Amazon, eBay, banggood and etsy?

WHY SHOPIFY IS THE BEST E-COMMERCE PLATFORM

First, let see what Wikipedia says about and the revenue generated as of 2017

Shopify is both a Canadian e-commerce company headquartered in Ottawa, Ontario and the name of its computer software platform *for online stores and retail point-of-sale systems.*

See the text bold and italic above.

That's cool, right?

Revenue as of 2017 - 151.7 million USD. This year 2018 will be hotter not to even talk of 2020 above

The number is insanely crazy, right?

Think of the profit Shopify store owner have already made

I believe you are seeing why Shopify is the best platform to start your e-commerce business

MORE REASON WHY SHOPIFY IS THE BEST PLATFORM

- Ability to retail Data

- Creating your own personal brand like Amazon, eBay and Etsy

- Physical store not require – everything online

-

- Work and run your business from home
- No age limit – ten-year-old can do this
- Easy to setup
- No technical skill require
- Partner with wholesaler
- Cool themes to install
- Work with big print on demand company like pillow profit and teelaunch
- Sell physical product
- Launch your own design e.g. t-shirt, pillow, shoe and so on
-

Worldwide shipping

-

Can be done anywhere in the world

The list is endless

Time will not permit me to emphasize more on the benefit of Shopify platform listed above

Now anyone can own a business and compete with a big brand.

Now that you know the benefit of Shopify, it's now time to start your own business and create your own brand

Chapter 2. How To Create Shopify Store

In this chapter, you will discover how easy it is to create and setup your Shopify store in less than 20 minutes.

You are one step away from owning your first brand and have a successful business that will replicate your day job. Keep reading

Creating Your Store

Now let jump into creating our store. Shopify has made it easy for everyone to setup their store with a free 14-day trial (https://goo.gl/t883bb)All you need to do now is to create your store with a 14-day trial using the link above

Now I assume you are on the page to create your store. Before creating your store making sure you read the niche and product research to choose your niche

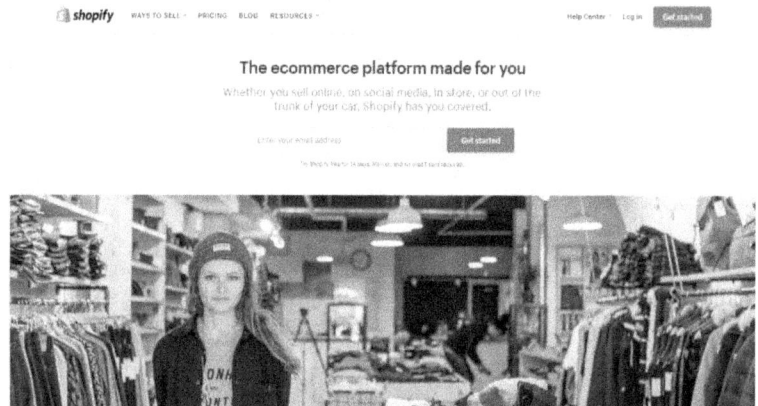

Step 1. Enter your email address and click get started

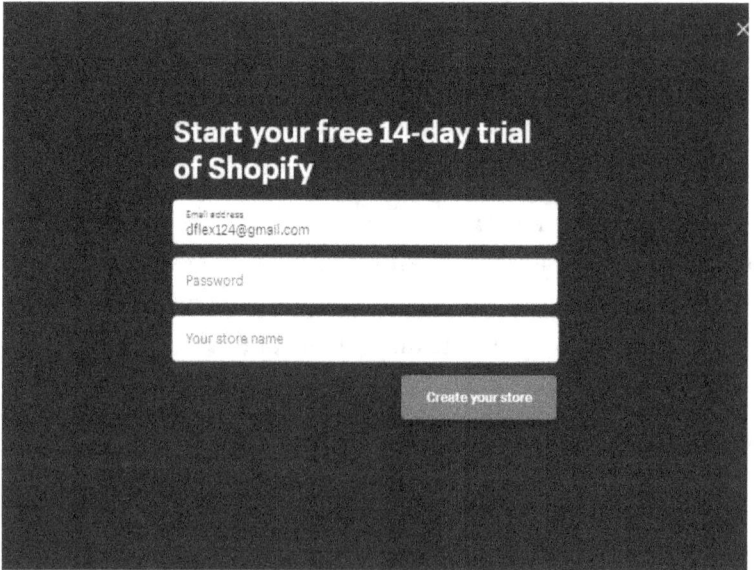

On this page, you want to input your detail, password and your store name. for example, assume am in the Dog niche, I will choose a name related to dog niche e.g. puppylover, dogarena, dog pup, lovepuppy and so on

After following the step and successfully created your Shopify store. You want to want to change the store currency to Dollar if you want to sell worldwide

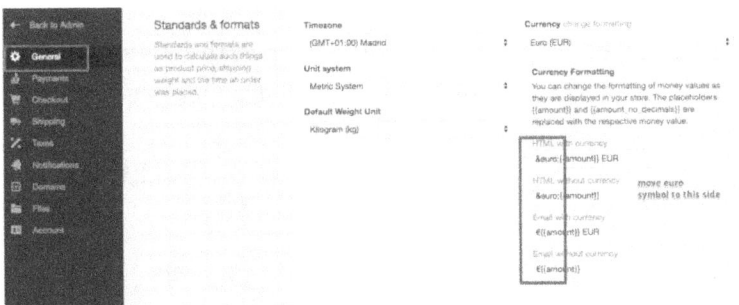

What you need to do next is to choose your theme, I will suggest you use the broklyn themes. It's completely free to use. Change the default image and set it to your own brand.

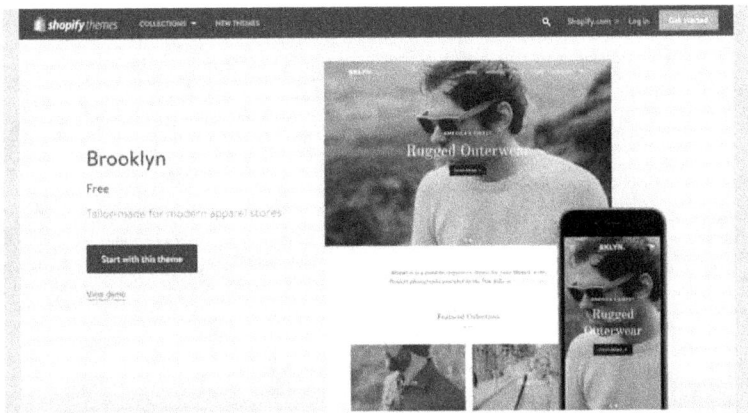

Play around with the theme to make it look professional. You can download the image from google to use but always make sure the image is label for reuse. To set the image to be reused from Google click the image, click more tools and click label for reuse from the drop-down menu. By following the step above you are protecting your store from copy Wright issue.

The next thing to do is to set the contact us page, return policy, terms and condition and privacy.

After setting up your store correctly, you need to study and master the next chapter because it's what you need to succeed in e-commerce.

Chapter 3. Niche And Product Research Strategy

This is the vital part of any online business especially when it comes to e-commerce. Without a perfect niche and product research strategy you will never succeed in the e-commerce business.

Niche and product research is the number key to succeed in e-commerce business and if you have been dreaming to create a brand and own a profitable online store that pull in $1000+ per day then you need to master this chapter very well because this is where your success lies.

If you can master this system alone you can control the money you make every single day and month.

Spending 3 to 4 hours per day searching and hunting for successful niche and product really worth it

In this chapter, I will review all you need to know in finding a successful niche and pick a winning product.

Keep reading!

Niche And Product Research With Etsy.com

Using Etsy for niche and product research is an effective way to know which niche and product will make you the most money as an ecom entrepreneur. If you can master this single giant e-commerce platform for niche and product research you don't need to start hunting for a winning product for your niche.

The reason is that after you find your niche, you will still have to carry out another research to find a winning product but Etsy take away the hard work of finding a niche and a winning product.

I called this a done for you system because all you have to do is to look at what others have done and duplicate other people success.

One more thing etsy does is that it show us who to target when running Facebook ads which is one of the cool things I love about Etsy.

The strategy I'm revealing in this book will never be found or seen elsewhere and most 8 figure e-commerce expert never review this method

Mastering Niche And Product Research With Etsy

- ✓ Step one. Go to etsy.com
- ✓ Step two. Input your niche keyword; e.g. unicorn
- ✓ Step three. Find the best selling product

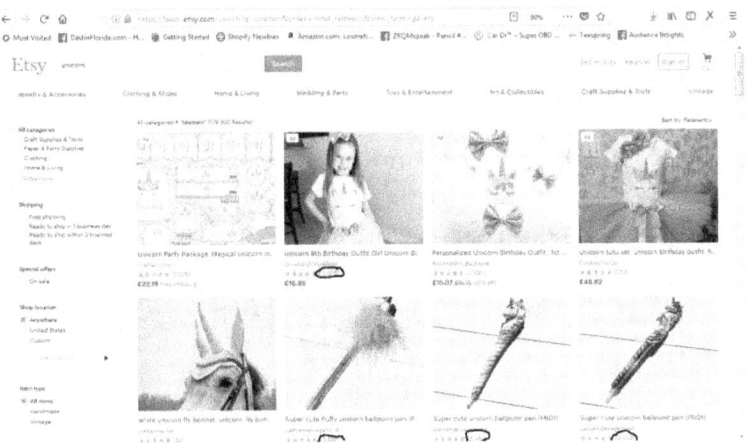

Now we find a product that is proven to convert from Etsy. Keynote: check product review with over 1000 review.

Now that we have found a winning product with Etsy the next thing is to go to the wholesaler platform I will review in the next chapter to find a similar product we can sell.

In the picture above, we find similar unicorn shirt (MARK WITH RED) that can replicate the same product from Etsy. The product is proven to sell and if marketed well, you can replicate the same success Etsy seller has. In chapter three I will show you the wholesaler platform I use to find a similar product from Etsy.

More Cool Feature From Etsy

- ✓ **Price point**: Etsy help us to know what price we should charge our product. When marketing your product, you don't need start testing price, all you have to do is to use the same price from Etsy seller
- ✓ **Targeting**: Another cool thing Etsy does is that it helps us know who are hungry for the product we are selling. All you have to do is to read through the comment

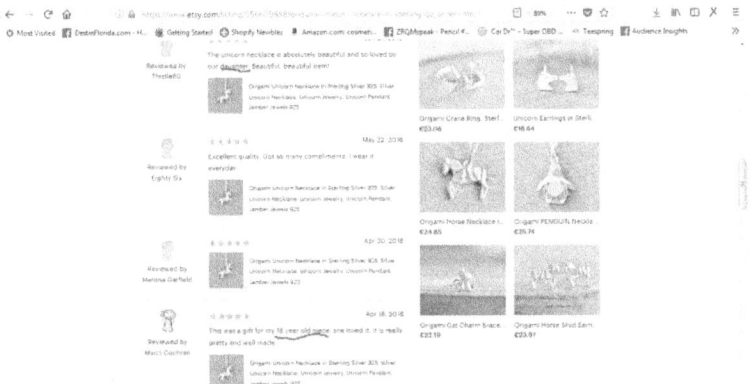

In the picture above, you will see clearly that the unicorn necklace is mainly bought for children which means when marketing through Facebook, the main people to target should be a parent under unicorn interest.

When creating your Facebook ads for the unicorn necklace. You can use this caption: THIS UNICORN NECKLACE IS PERFECT FOR YOUR KIDS.

> Step four. Find more hot product from seller store: when you find your favorite niche and product from Etsy, you want to find more product by clicking the seller store. this strategy will help you find more done for you product that is proven to sell.

Niche And Product Research With Exchange.shopify.com

Exchange.shopify.com: This platform is created by Shopify and its main feature is for selling and buying Shopify store. If you grow a store with Shopify store you can list the store for sale on this platform.

The cool thing about Exchange.shopify.com is that it's a great tool to spy on successful and profitable Shopify store.

All you have to do is to head over to Shopify exchange

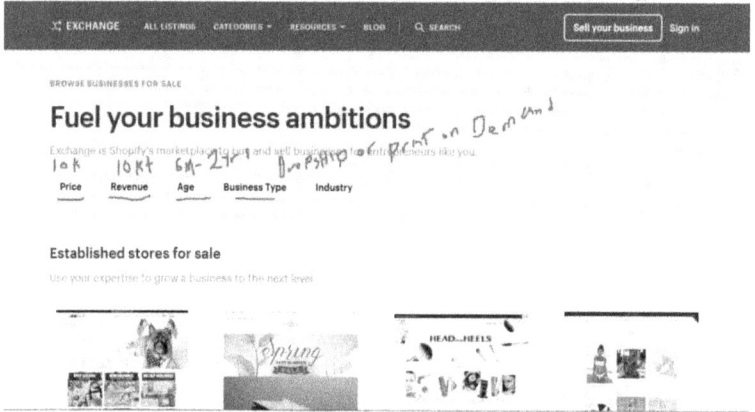

Check the feature site or filter the site just as you see above and below to get a great result.

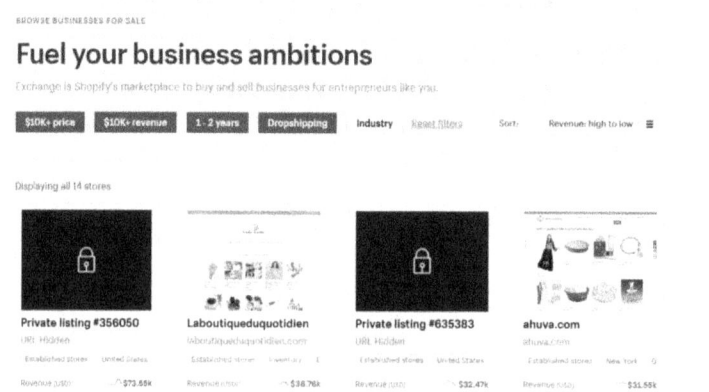

Start clicking and checking over the site. After finding a site that performed well, all you need to do is to do the exact thing they have done. Import the same product or similar product they are selling to your store. You can check what they are posting on the social network to know how and when they share their content.

What you need to do next is to subscribe to their email list to know what kind of content and when they sent out a mail to their entire list.

NICHE AND PRODUCT RESEARCH WITH MYIP.MS

This is another great tool to spy on profitable Shopify store. It combines over **100,288** successful Shopify store. Spending over 1 to 2 hours hunting for a niche to start a new store around really worth.

All you have to do is to head over to this [site](#) right now to discover new profitable store and duplicate what they have done. Follow the step below to get started

- Step one. Go to [myip.ms](#)
- Step two. Go to google.com and enter "Shopify IP address" into the search box

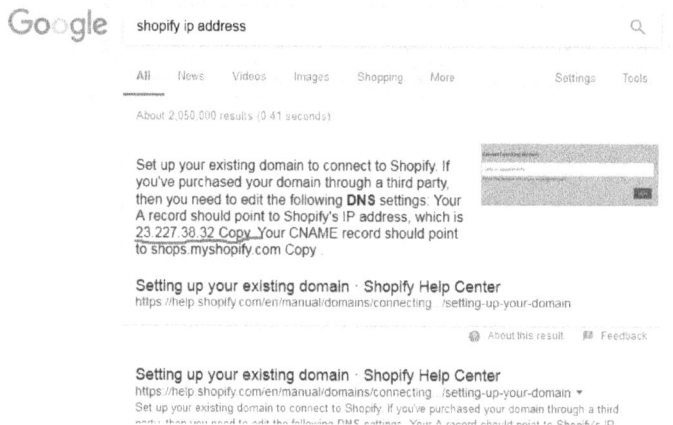

Copy the highlighted link and past in my myip.ms

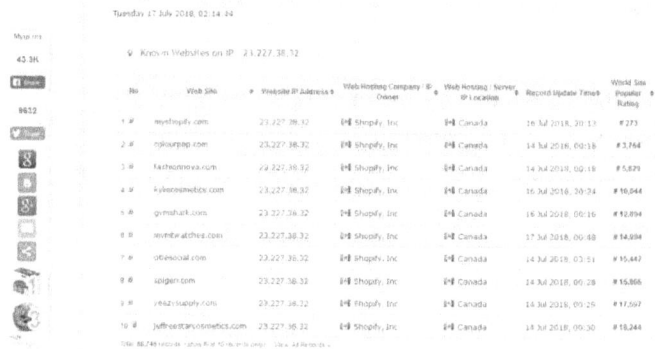

Now you can start clicking on over 100k+ successful Shopify store to know what they are selling that made them more successful.

NICHE AND PRODUCT RESEARCH WITH GOOGLE TREND

Google trend is one of the best tools out there to know what is hot right now. It a tool created by Google. If you want to know which niche to go into, I will suggest you use google trend. It will help you know what people are searching in a chart format. With this tool, you will know when a keyword is trending and when it's descending. Again it will let you know whether or not to go with a niche or not.

Let see whether the unicorn niche is a great niche to create a store around

When using google trend I like to filter my search to the following.

- ➢ Change worldwide to the United State
- ➢ Change past 12 months to Past 90 Day,
- ➢ Change all category to Shopping

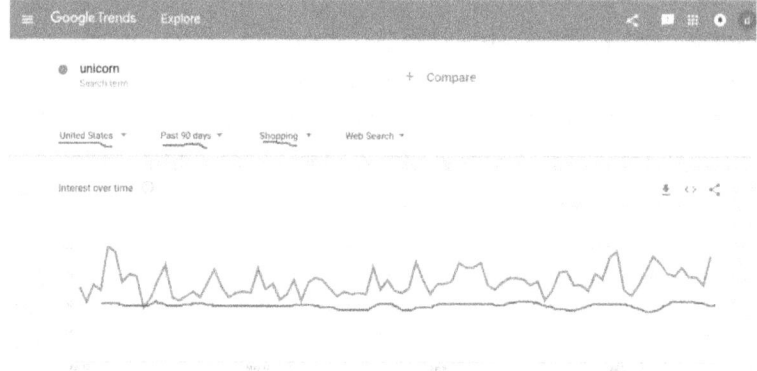

From the result above, we can see clearly that unicorn niche is a profitable niche we can create store around because the interest is above 50%. If the interest is below %50 don't bother to go for that niche because it not a profitable niche. See the picture below for a non-profitable product

In the picture above we can see clearly the interest for the fidget spinner is below %50 which shows that people are not searching for the product right now. Creating a store around

fidget spinner is a complete waste of time. So it better to avoid that kind of product entirely.

Note, when starting for a new store always make use of google trend to know whether people are searching for the product. If the interest is above %50 it a good niche but if it's below %50 don't go for that niche.

MORE FEATURE OF GOOGLE TREND

Google trend is not only meant for searching what is trending alone, it also helps us to know the region and city that is searching for the niche and product we are selling on our store. See the picture below for an example

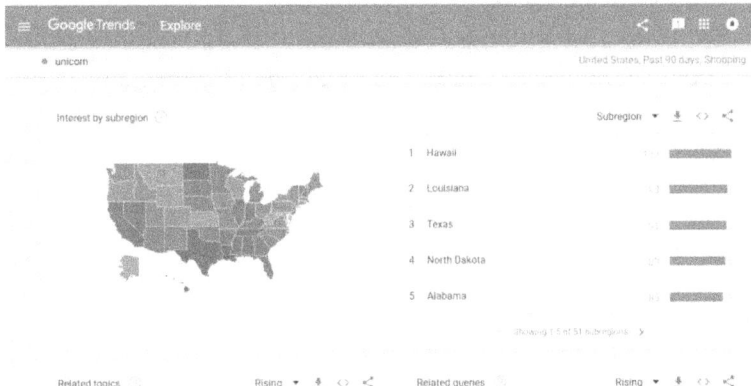

From the picture above, I know the exact region to target when running my facebook ads

NICHE AND PRODUCT RESEARCH WITH FACEBOOK

Facebook is one of the best tools out there that show exactly what is happening to a product in a specific niche. With Facebook, we will be able to detect whether a product is performing well or not by seeing the impression e.g. Likes, Shares, and Comments

To get started with Facebook, go to facebook.com and enter some phrase below

- ✓ Goo.gl + niche or product name e.g. goo.gl unicorn

Actionable step

- ✓ Click the video section
- ✓ Click on most watch video
- ✓ Create similar video or download and edit the video
- ✓ Upload

More search phrase

- ✓ Buy now unicorn

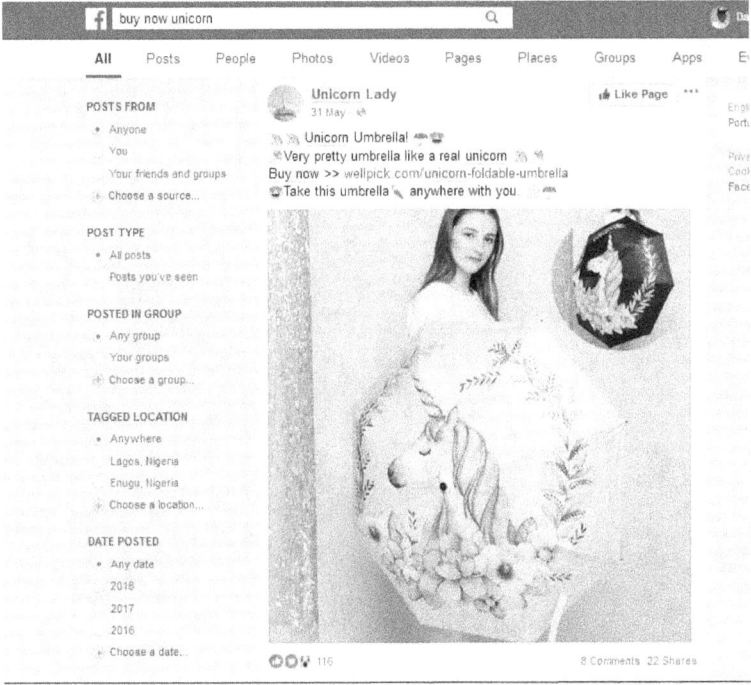

Now you can see that typing the word 'buy now unicorn' have discovered that unicorn umbrella is a good product to start selling because of the impression.

All you need to do is scroll down and click on SEE ALL in PUBLIC POST section

See more product I discover when I clicked on to see all section

Public posts

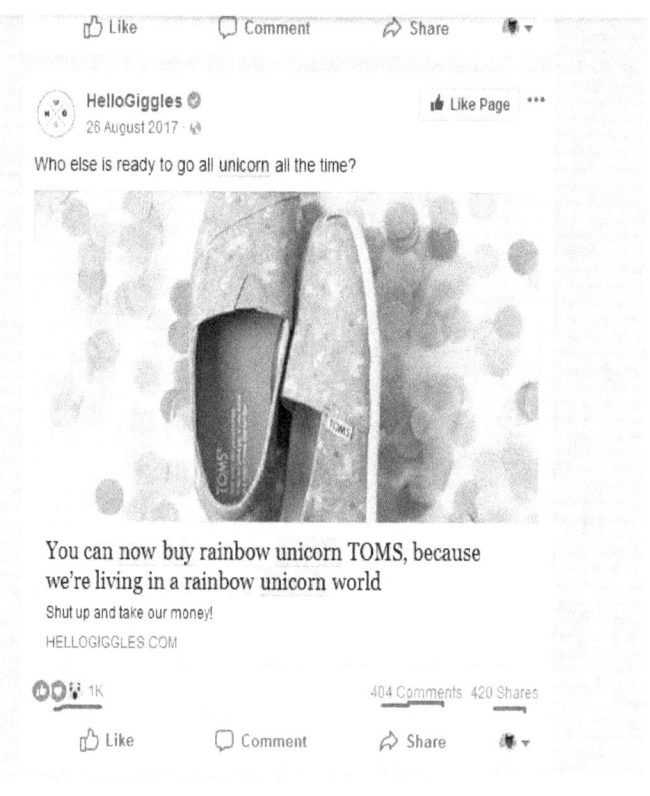

Public posts

With the impression each product above have, am well convinced that products will perform well and are already proven to generate sales. You can narrow down your search by entering this search phrase.

Buy now + niche (unicorn) + product (ring or necklace or umbrella or bracelet or t-shirt e.t.c.).

- ✓ Get yours now
- ✓ Free shipping

Make sure you narrow down your search using the example above

How To Effectively Use Amazon.com

Amazon is the giant e-commerce platform so it a great thing to spy on Amazon to know how the product is performing.

Amazon is mostly used to finalize the result derived from each research made. This simply means that if a product performed well on Amazon, the product is proven to convert better on our store. See example below

Little Girls Gift – Fantasy – 5/8 Inch 15MM Disc – Customize Name – Choose Birthstone Color – Fast 1 Day Shipping

 111 customer reviews
| 7 answered questions

There is every tendency that this product is going to perform well.

ALWAYS MAKE USE OF WATCHCOUNT

Watchcount is another great and powerful tool to know if a product is performing well or not

What this tool does is that it give you the ability to look over a product and look how many people are watching over that product

Watchcount is powered by eBay and every dropshipper must effectively make use of this platform.

Take for example, if you find a product that over 500 above people are watching on, what did you think? Did you think the owner of that product generates sales or not?

Absolutely yes and if a product that has over 500 plus does not generate a sale, that means there is a problem with that store

HOW TO USE WATCHCOUNT FOR FINDING A WINNING PRODUCT

Simply open your browser and go to watchcount.com

Enter your keyword e.g. unicorn.

Now below we can see different product idea we can sell under unicorn niche

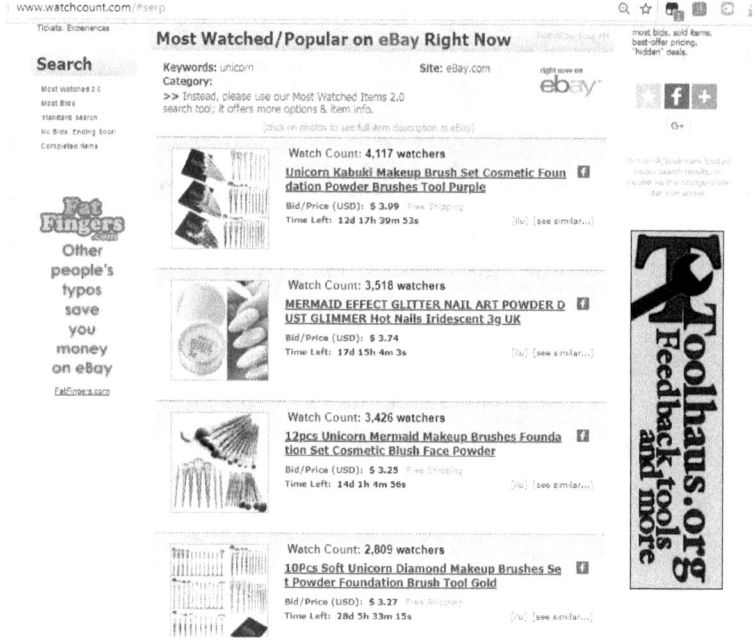

If you scroll down this page you will find several unicorn products you can sell in your store. All you need to do is to import that product from aliexpress to your store.

What you can next is to narrow down your keyword by entering the **niche + product** to see how product is performing well. See example below

- Unicorn ring
- Unicorn necklace
- Unicorn bracelet
- Unicorn umbrella
- Unicorn top
- Unicorn sneaker
- Unicorn cloth

- Unicorn phone case
- Unicorn baby cloth

And so on.

Let see on more example

- Unicorn baby cloth

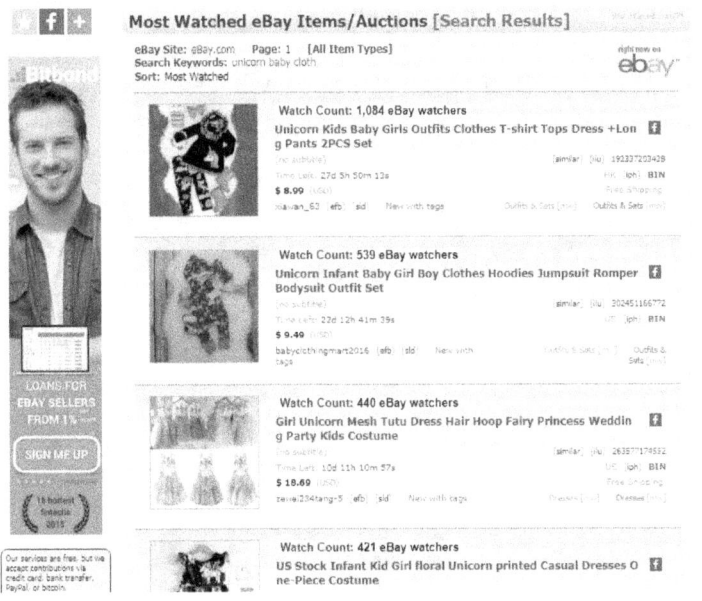

Now we can see that over 1000 people are watching the first unicorn baby cloth.

With the research being done for a unicorn, now we can come to a conclusion that unicorn product will perform well.

Because we find the unicorn cosmetics selling for $3.99 in watchcount doesn't mean that will sell it for that same price.

Here is the couple of things I will do with the product.

I can sell the product as a

- Give the product away and charge for shipping (F + S) product at $7.99 or $9.99
- charge shipping at $4.95 or $3.99 and sell the product for $5 or $6
- offer free shipping and charge the product for $10.99 or $14.99 or look another store online to see what they are charging for cosmetics product.

All you need to is test different price to see which one work better for you.

Chapter 4. Best Platform To Find Supplier

After finding a niche and product, the next step is to find the right platform to get the supplier to deliver your product to your customer whenever you make a sales.

The two platforms I will recommend is ALIEXPPRESS.COM and DHGATE.COM

If you are looking to sell a heavy product like a generator, electric massaging chair or any product you cannot find on the two listed platform above, you can use ALIBABA but the problem with most Alibaba supplier is that they don't support dropshipping. All you have to do is to contact them to know if they can dropship your product to your customer. If they can't dropship your product then you need to move on and if they agree to dropship your product you can move on.

Also if you want to own an inventory or do AMAZON FBA, ALIBABA is the right platform to use.

Aliexpress For Dropshipping

Aliexpress is the best platform to find dropshipper who are ready to ship your product to the entire world whenever you make a sale. All you need to do is to go to the site and enter the product name you are winning to sell or discover from your research.

From the previous research (etsy) in the chapter, we discover a product that is already proven to work. See the Picture below

We can see clearly that we are able to find a similar product from aliexpress that we can sell at the same price as Etsy and still profit.

This is how to find a product to sell in your store. If the product is not the same, it will look similar to that product you discover from your research.

HOW TO FIND A GOOD SUPPLIER

When finding a product to dropship to your store, always filter your search from BEST MATCH to ORDERS.

If you find a product you're searching for, check the seller rating and feedback. See picture below

Hover your cursor to the section I mark with red or scroll down to the review section to see the seller review and feedback. The seller above is an example of a good dropshipper. When selecting a product to import to your store, make sure the seller support Epacket for shipping

DHGATE.COM FOR DROPSHIPPING

Dhgate is another great platform to find a supplier that is willing to dropship your product. This platform is similar to aliexpress and is also good for dropshipping.

When hosting your store with Shopify, aliexpress is the best platform to use to dropship because of the apps to import your product to Shopify with just a click of a button

Chapter 5. Best Apps For Importing Product

Now that we have our store setup, the next thing is to find an app to dropship the product from aliexpress to Shopify store. The Shopify importing apps I will be revealing in this chapter do not only allow us to import the product to our store but also allow us to buy the product with a click of a button from aliexpress saving us the time of inputting customer address manually on aliexpress.

Oberlo Apps For Importing And Fulfilling Order

Oberlo app is the ever best apps for importing and fulfilling the order on Shopify.

Installing on Shopify

To install this app on our store, all you have to do is to click on the apps section on Shopify and input oberlo apps in the search box

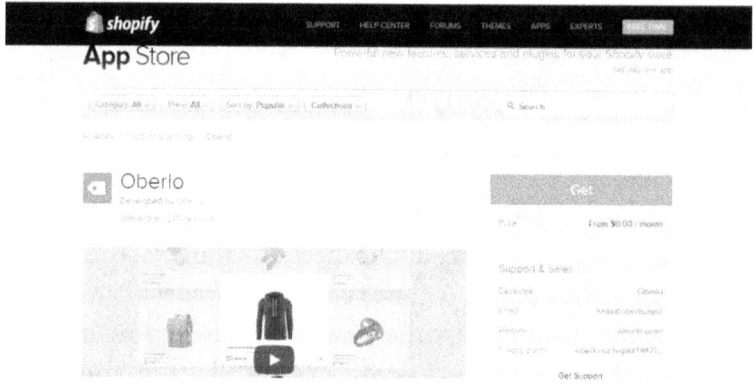

Once found, click Get button and follow the step to install the app on your store

IMPORTING AND FULFILLING ORDER

To product to Shopify store from aliexpress can be done with a click of a button. To get this done, we need to install oberlo chrome extension. Follow the guide below to install oberlo chrome extension successfully for importing product to your Shopify store

INSTALLING OBERLO ON GOOGLE CHROME
Go to google.com

Enter this search phrase 'oberlo chrome extension' click on the first result from google and install

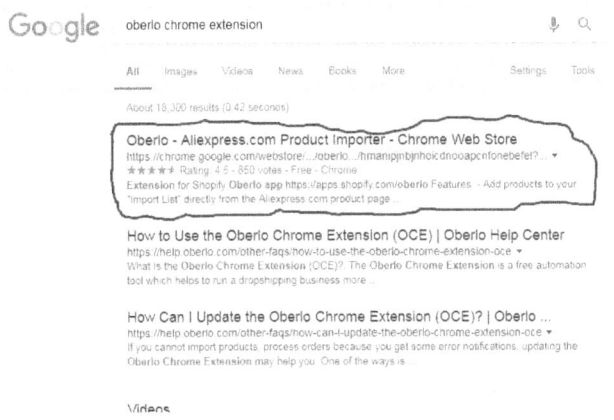

If successfully installed, it will look exactly like this on aliexpress

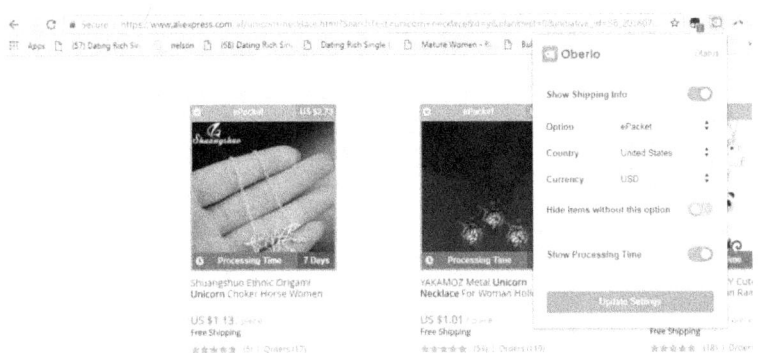

From the picture above, we can see clearly that the app is already found in chrome and also on aliexpress. All you need to do is to hover your mouse on the product and oberlo click on oberlo icon that appears to import the product. In less than seconds you will find the product on your oberlo dashboard, what you need to next is to edit the product title and description and click publish and your product will be live on your store.

Note; always import the product with the epacket alone.

FULFILLING ORDER

Once a sale is made, in less than 20 seconds you can fulfill your order with just a click of a button. All you need to do is to click on oberlo apps from your Shopify store and login to your dashboard to fulfill the order

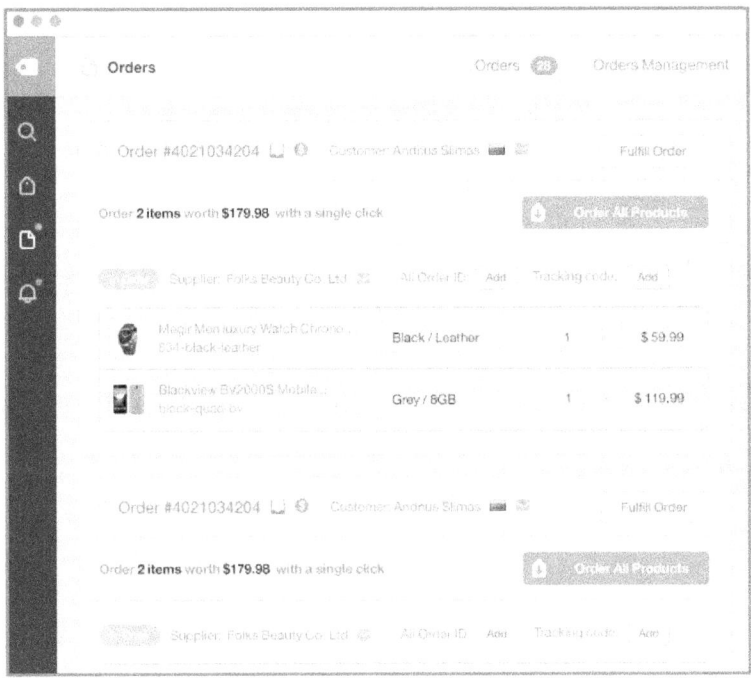

Now you can fulfill your order with a click of a button. one next thing you can do to fulfill the order is outsourcing.

With outsourcing, you can hire someone to fulfill orders while you focus your attention on finding a winning product and marketing your product to generate more sales.

Finding someone to fulfill your order is easy, all you need to do is go to upwork.com to find freelancer willing to do your job for you.

One last thing you need to take note when fulfilling the order is that you have to contact your supplier and inform them that you are dropshipping this product to your customer. Tell them not to include any form of promo in the product when delivering the product to your customer. You can either inform them to blind dropship the product or ask them if they can print (this may cause additional charges but very effective for building a brand) the logo of your business on the packages.

Go with the blind dropship if you are just starting up or if you don't have enough money to invest in the printing package

Chapter 6. Other App To Increase Sale

At this point I believe we have learned a lot from creating a store, spying o profitable Shopify store, perfect niche and product research with Facebook, Etsy niche and product research, best wholesaler platform and best apps to import and fulfill the order.

Learning and mastering the step above is the key to success in Shopify dropshipping. If you are to read the four chapter above more than 4 times to master the system, go and do it because it's the vital part you need to succeed in e-commerce especially the niche and product research strategy.

I believe you understood what I discuss perfectly in the previous chapter, if you did not I will huge you to retake and master it before studying further. Now let discuss more apps to increase Shopify store

Top 3 Apps To Increase Shopify Store

The apps I will review in this chapter will help in increasing our profit and make our Shopify store look busy when sale start rolling in

ABANDONMENT PROTECTOR PLUS

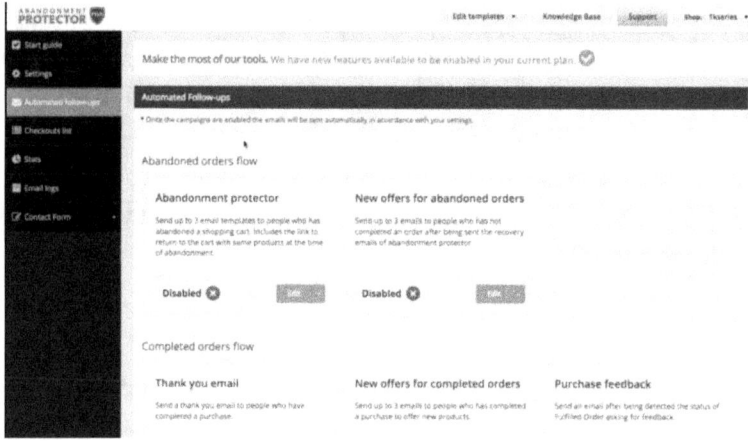

This apps is a must have on your store. If you have a store and you don't have this app on your store, you are definitely losing tons of money and living money on the table. This app can help you generate extra 10,000 dollars from your store. What this app does is that it send a message to anyone that abandon their cart and bring them back to your store to complete their purchase. The cool thing about this app is that you can send up to three different message for reminding people to complete their purchase. This is done for you strategy, all you need to do is set it once and the app takes care of the rest.

Follow the simple guide below to set up this app

- ✓ In the above picture, click on EDIT in the ABANDONMENT PROTECTOR section
- ✓ Click on Edit Email Templates

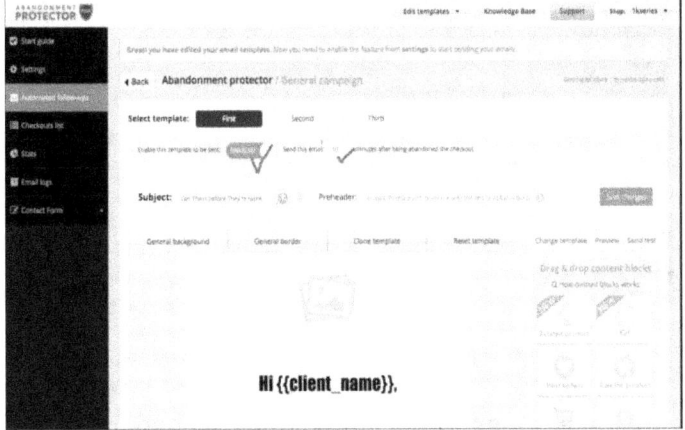

On the next page (sample above) click on Enable and leave the time set to 10 minutes after checkout has been abandon. Enable the other two to send out an email if the customer didn't complete their order. All you need to do is to choose a different template and set the second time to either 3 or 5 hours while the third should be set to either 15 or 20 hours depending on your choice. You need to set up this app on your store to maximize your revenue.

SALES POP BY BEEKETING

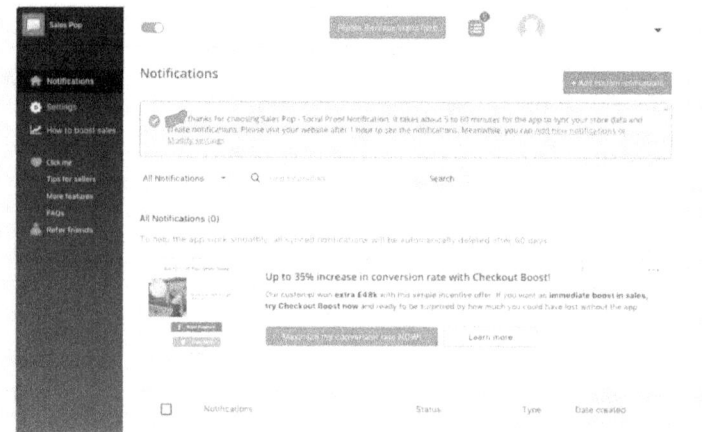

This app makes the Shopify store look busy and increase the conversion rate on our store. All you need to do is to install the apps on your store and turn it on.

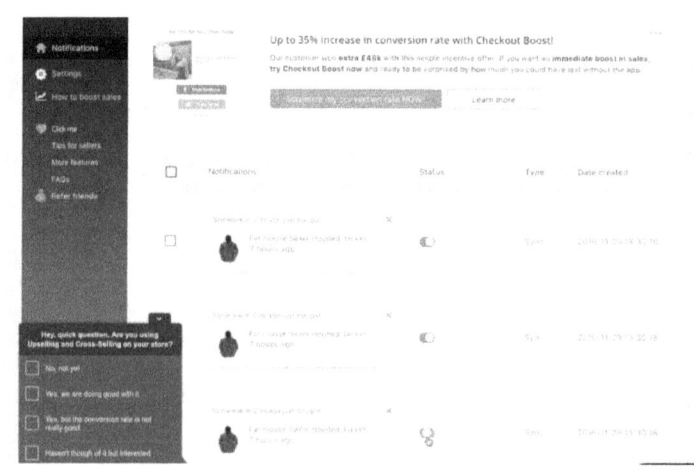

Once you successfully setup this app on your store it will start popping (notification) up item sold on your store and increase social proof.

HURRIFY – COUNTDOWN TIMER

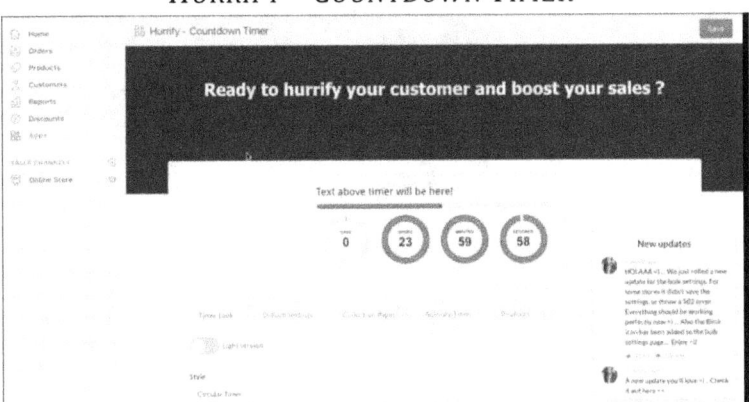

Hurrify timer is another great Shopify app you should have in every of your store. What this app does is that it helps increase urgency and makes every customer sent to your store act fast. Install this app on your store and follow the guide below to set this app up on your store.

Style – simple timer 1 and click save

Step two – click on the product

Click on select all products to add this timer to every single product on your store

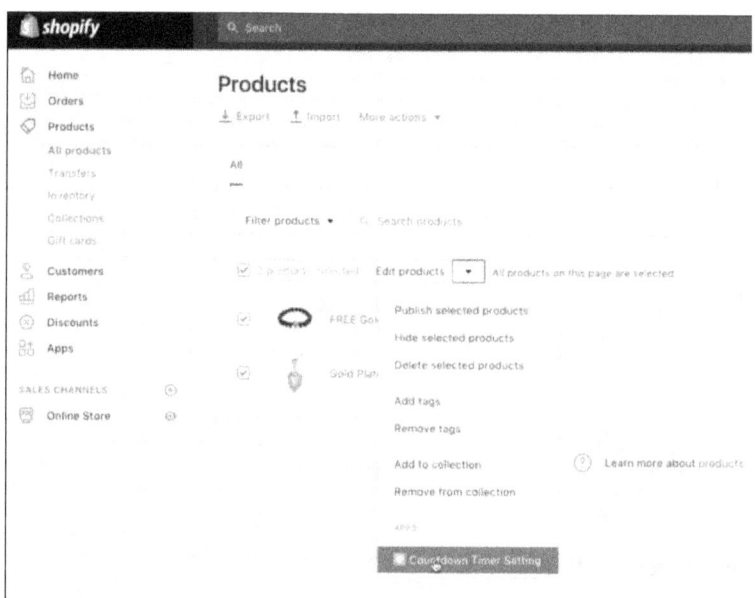

On the next page, all you need to do is to enable this timer and click save. Set the timer to either 12 hours or any of your choice

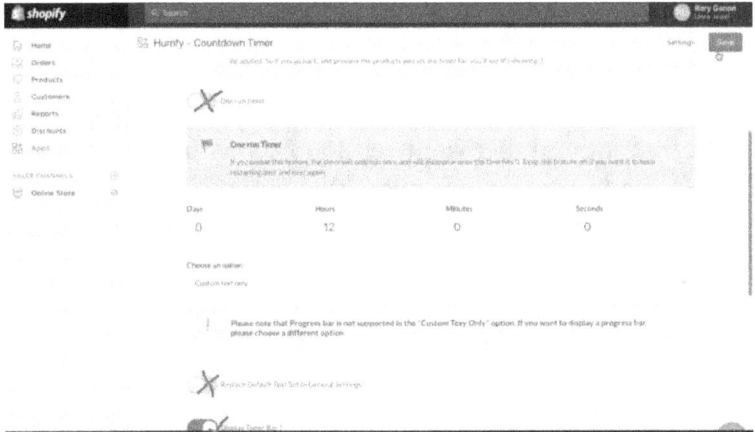

Once you follow the step above. Go to your store and click on a product to see how it look like

.

The picture above is a sample of how the timer will appear on each product.

Chapter 7. How To Write Title And Description And Product pricing

This is the major area that you need to focus your attention on. Your description most at time will tell if someone will buy from you or not due to this you need to focus 60 percent of your time in writing your description. One more thing is that the description must be short and precise and must able to create urgency and scarcity.

Formatting Title

You need to format your product title to make it personal. You want to avoid using the exact title from aliexpress. When writing your title, remove the brand name and keep the title short.

Description

These are a few things you need to do when writing your product title.

- ✓ Urgency; this offer won't last long, Customer is going crazy over this product
- ✓ Scarcity; e.g. only a few lefts in stock, we sell out fast,
- ✓ Tell a short story about the product
- ✓ Write why people should buy the product e.g. if am selling a sunglasses then I will let people know the problem of not wearing eyeglass during the sun and why they need to wear the sunglass to prevent the eyes from sunset.
- ✓ Edit the product specification from aliexpress by deleting the brand name and some specific detail pertaining to the brand
- ✓ Edit product image if they brand logo appear on the image

PRODUCT PRICING

Pricing is another thing to take note so you won't scare the customer away with the price you are charging your product.

If you are selling similar product from Etsy then you can use their exact price but if you are selling a product that is not from Etsy you need to browse the similar website and check the price they are charging for that product

You can either add or reduce the price if you wish and as far you still make a profit from your product then you can reduce or add money to the product

SHIPPING TIME

Don't be scared to mention the shipping time in your description. Long shipping time doesn't mean that your customer will not buy your product.

Since we are using epacket for delivering the product, always let the customer know that the product will take 12 to 25 day before their product will arrive.

CHAPTER 8. MARKETING INTRO

The following chapter is the holy grail of making money from your store. The following chapter is what will help you in creating a real brand through the social network. After setting up your store successfully then will need to drive traffic to it before anything can happen if there is no traffic, absolutely there is no going to be any sale and nobody will know whether our store is in existence

MARKETING

Let talk little about marketing. In every business, marketing is what will detect a business growth

What is marketing: in my own term, marketing can be defined as a way of creating product awareness to a specific region or area and presenting the product in a way that will make people take quick and urgent action in purchasing the product.

Without effective marketing, you will never hit the level of success you are looking for.

You need to focus on marketing almost all your product to find a winning product. If you find a winning product the next thing is to scale fast and kill other products that are not performing well.

If you can master the method of marketing below then you can control your income the income you make every single day.

TRAFFIC

I will start this chapter with this quote; whoever can spend a money to acquire a customer win. That's the fact

Traffic is the livelihood of any online business, without this, you are not going to reach anywhere. So you need to focus your attention on driving traffic to your store

TWO WAY TO GET TRAFFIC

Below are the two way to drive traffic to your store. The first one is scalable, fast and consistency but requires investment while the other one is considered to be a long time process to get traffic to your website

- ✓ Paid traffic; this is the fastest way to drive multiple people to your site. These kinds of traffic are targeted and are meant to generate result fast. E.g. if am marketing a dog product I can simply target those who are a dog lover. This kind of advert can be done on google adword, youtube ads, solo ads and Facebook ads

- ✓ Free traffic; this kind of traffic takes time and effort and are not fast in getting result require. You can get this kind of traffic from doing a guest blog, posting on the forum, posting and commenting on the facebook group

Now that we know the different way of driving traffic to your online store. Let go to the next chapter to start learning the various way to market our product and in chapter 11, I review one secret source to get fast free traffic to our store

Chapter 9. Influencer Marketing

Influencer marketing is one of the cheapest ways to start marketing your product online to the same audience meaning influencer marketing is a well-targeted traffic. You can start this type of marketing for as low as $10 above and reach thousands of like-minded people who are hungry for your product

Below are the different site you can get started with influencer marketing

Instagram Influencer Marketing

This is the best way to get targeted traffic to your online store for as low as $10 upward. With this marketing system, you can get your product in front of over 100k to 1M likeminded people in less than 24 hours. Below is the exact way you can find a good influencer that makes you more than $1000 above

How To Identify Good And Bad Instagram Influencer

When starting with an Instagram influencer, you need to be very careful in selecting influencer to work with because most Instagram influencers has a fake follower. They only have multiple followers but those followers are not profitable because they buy follower and not gaining a real follower.

GOOD INFLLUENCER

- ✓ Go to instagram.com
- ✓ Type your niche in the search box e.g. lion
- ✓ Check site that has the most like and comment

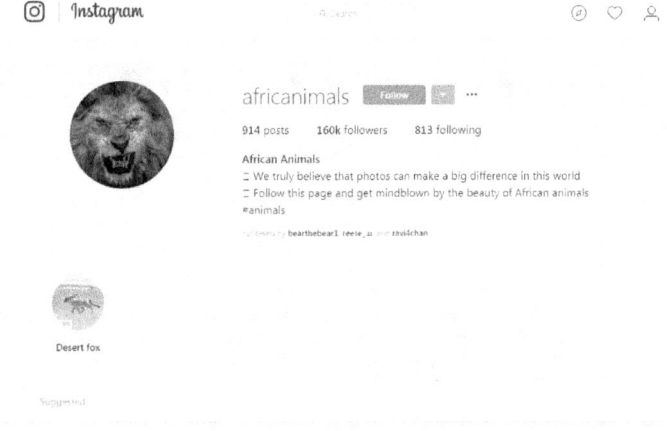

This site has over 160k like which is quite impressing but again, like doesn't matter here is the level of engagement that we are looking at.

Most images on this page has over 10k plus like with over 50+ comment.

- ✓ Check the comment whether they have a genuine comment.

- ✓ Go to socialblade.com to know if they are gaining or buying follower. Chose Instagram from the dropdown and copy past username (africanimals) to the search box

- ✓ Scroll and see the result. If they are getting 1000+ like with A or B+ sign it good to go with

This influencer is not that much good to go with but can still run a promotion with them because the result above shows that they are gaining good follower and not buying follower.

The comment on this influencer page is genuine. Running promotion with this kind of page is okay but getting a follower that get 1000 plus follower with A and B plus sign will be extremely profitable

- ✓ Refresh the Instagram page after 2 or 3 hours and see if they are still getting like. If they get like, run your ads with them but if they didn't get any like, search for another influencer or give them a try

Note: make sure it's their newest post to know if they are still getting like after 2 – 3 hours

PRICING AND NEGOTIATING WITH INFLUENCER

One thing you want to avoid is overpaying the Instagram influencer. E.g. paying $80 to $100 plus for the influencer page above is totally wrong. They might charge you something like that but you always ways want to contact them back and negotiate the price. Always negotiate with the influencer. For the page above, I will only pay them $20 to $35 for promoting my product on their page.

They might say your promo will last on their page for 2 or 1 week but always tell them you want your post to last for either 12 or 24 hours because your sales will come in the next 12 hours. By making them understand this, they will lower their charges.

Note: always run your promo for 12 or 24 hours. Don't go for one week above promo.

HOW TO PITCH INSTAGRAM INFLUENCER

Knowing the right way to contact the influencer will let you get quick feedback from an influencer.

You can reach influencer fast by contacting them with their email or Kik messenger. Again whenever you send an email to their email address or message them on kik messenger you always want to DM them on their Instagram page letting them know that you sent them a message to their email or Kik messenger

Here are the few messages you can send to influencer

- ✓ Hello (Instagram name), I will like to promote my product on your Instagram page, what is your rate?

- ✓ Hello, my friend parker will like to promote their lion jewel on your Instagram page, how can we get started?

At the end of your message, always end your message with MY REGARD.

YOUR NAME

HOPING TO HEAR FROM YOU FAST

That's all you need to do to contact Instagram influencer

CREATING YOUR PROMO FOR INSTAGRAM INFLUENCER

After coming to an agreement with the influencer, you need to create the image and the caption you will send to the influencer to post on their page

Note: always create your Instagram page to get this done. Never put a link on the influencer page by creating your page you will gain more followers.

By doing so you are creating a social brand and online presence for your online store.

To create your Instagram image, always use a company called canva.com to create your image. Set the px for 800px * 800px

Upload the image you want to use for the promo and input words and emoji. See below for some image I created for Instagram influencer

FREE BRACELET

Free Make Up Brush - Just Pay Shipping

The ads above are an example on how you can create an Instagram image for the influencer. This is just an Idea on how to create your ads for the Instagram sponsored post.

When writing your caption for Instagram influencer, you can check other promo on another influencer page to get an idea of what to say but you can say something like this.

- ✓ OMG! Are you a dog lover? We are giving away this dog necklace completely free to 10 or 50 (influencer page name) followers for the next 12 hours only. Hurry and Get yours now, only a few lefts to be given away. Click the link in our bio to get yous now

- ✓ In opening our store, we are giving away this dog necklace to 10 followers to (page name you're are running the promo) for the next 12 hour. Click Link in our bio to claim your free god paw necklace

Note: choose a number. This will help create urgency and scarcity for the product you are promoting on influencer page and will make people take massive action in purchasing your product.

OTHER INFLUENCER MARKETING PLATFORM

You can try this other influencer marketing platform listed below to get targeted traffic to your store

- ✓ Twitter influencer marketing: use socialblade to see how their getting their followers and contact them if they will promote your product on your page

- ✓ Youtube influencer: get in touch with the youtube influencer to know if they will promote your product in the next video they will upload on their page. The problem with the youtube influencer is that they charge way too far but always negotiate the price they charge. Ask them to mention your product in their description and link back to your store.

Chapter 10. Facebook Marketing

Facebook is the number one social media platform with over **1.45 billion** active users visit daily. What does that mean to your business? If you are not using Facebook to market your product you are leaving thousands of money on the table

Almost all the human being is on Facebook today so if you are not using Facebook right now you need to start using facebook today because your audience is waiting for you to show your product to them.

You seriously want to focus 90% of your time marketing your product on Facebook.

If you master Facebook marketing alone, you can make thousands and millions of dollars focusing on this platform alone

Follow the below guide to create your first Facebook ads

Before you start creating your ads or driving any traffic to your store through facebook and influencer marketing, make sure to install facebook pixel on your store so facebook can track everything going on in your store

STEP BY STEP TO FACEBOOK MARKETING

- ✓ Log in to facebook ads manager
- ✓ Click the Create ads button
- ✓ Click on conversions and name your campaign

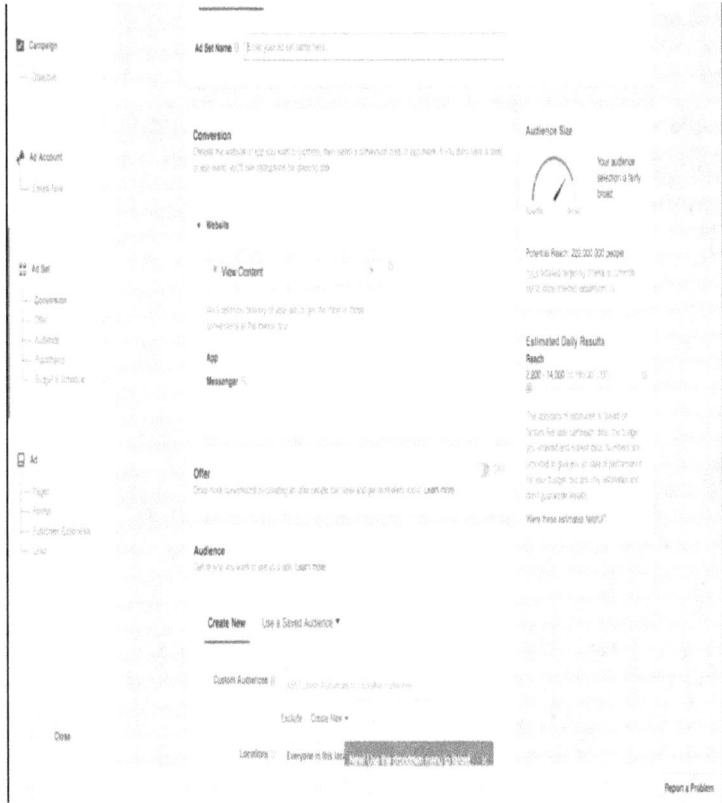

Note that we are optimizing for conversion for purchase

- ✓ change the View Content to Purchase
- ✓ choose location

While choosing a location, you can use the top three location from google trend

- ✓ you want to change the age from 18+ to 21+

Reason from choosing the 21+ above is that most people within the age of 18 don't have money to purchase items online

- ✓ Age – 21 to 50. See reason below
- ✓ Gender – woman. See reason below

To know the gender to choose, go to facebook ads insight

What facebook ads insight does is that it show us everything about the interest we are looking for. Always use facebook insight to know which gender and interest to choose. On the facebook insight choose Everyone On Facebook

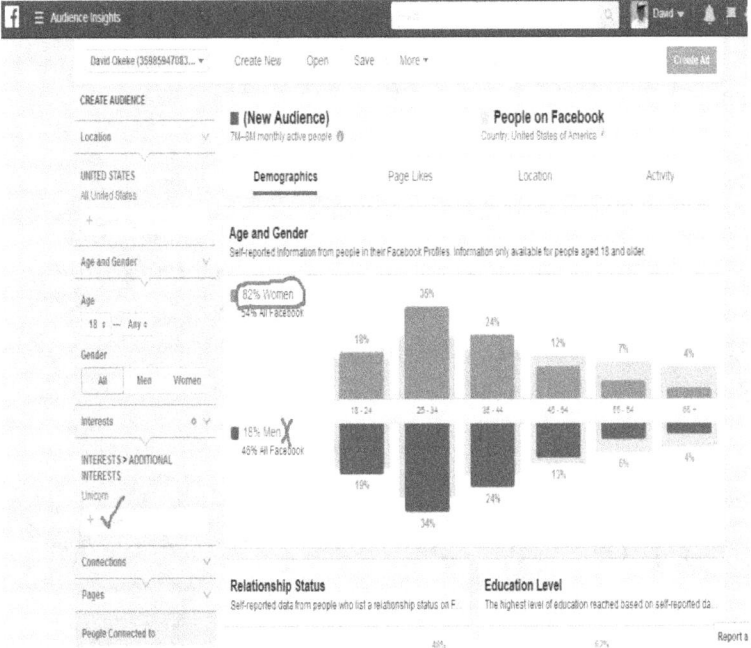

From the above result, you can see clearly that I type unicorn as in interest and Facebook quickly scan the demographic and tell me the age and gender of those who have the most interest for a unicorn. From the picture above 82% of woman have interest for a unicorn and 18% of men have an interest in a unicorn. In the age section in my facebook ads, I will choose 21 – 50.

✓ In the audience section

Type your keyword and Facebook will give you similar interest. See the killer interest below to target under the unicorn niche

Chose from similar interest from a unicorn or use the suggestion on facebook insight by clicking on Page Likes and opening each page to see if it similar to the interest you are looking for. If it's similar, copy the name of the page and paste it in the interest section.

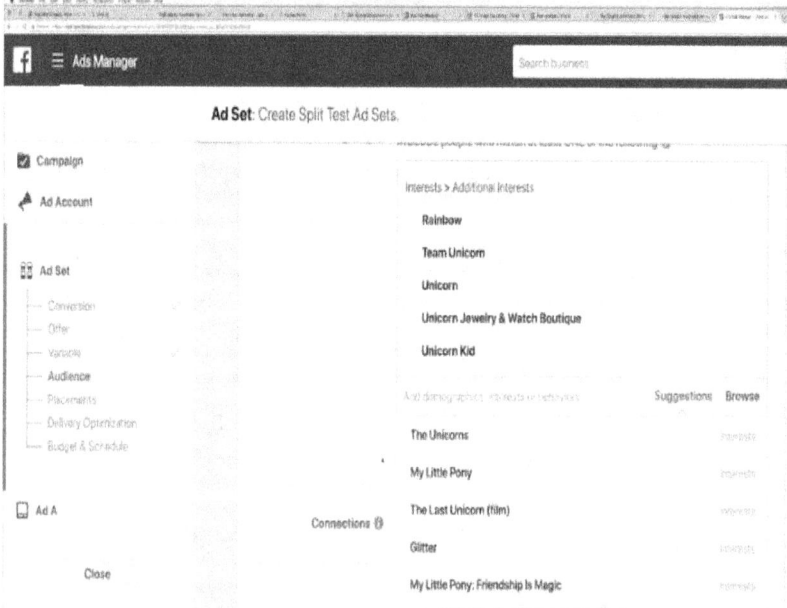

- ✓ Placement – chose edit placement

In this section we only want our ads to appear in the facebook newsfeed. Due to that, we will uncheck all the other placement. See the image below

Note; Only chose newsfeed for ad placement

- ✓ Budget - $5 or $10 per day

While choosing your budget, it ok to start with $5 per day budget or $10 per day but I will suggest $5 per day at first.

Study how your ad is performing!! If the ads are not showing the good result after 4 to 5 days, KILL it fast to avoid losing money but if the ads are doing great, meaning sales is coming in. scale from $5 to $10 above per day.

- ✓ Pages – in the page section you want to select your business (fan) page you created for the niche you are into. If you haven't created a fan page, you can create one to continue your ads

- ✓ Format, full-screen experience and link – first thing to do when you get to this section is to upload your ads image. To create your ads, use canva.com and select pixel size to **1,200 x 628 pixels.**

Chose your **fan page** in the **identity** section

Chose a **single image** in the **format section** to upload your image

Download the product image you want to use, upload and customize it with some text. See example below

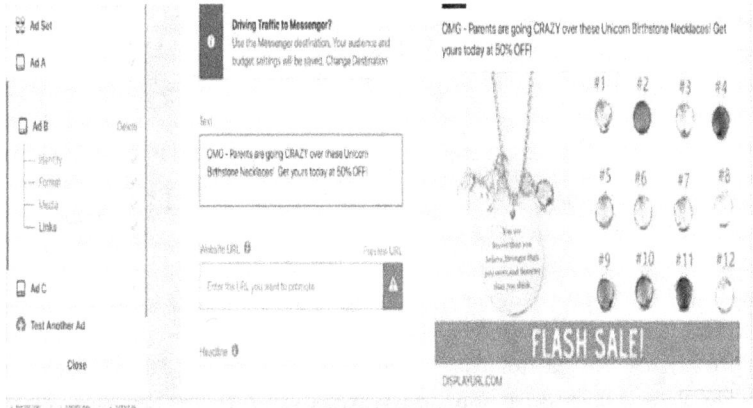

Now, our ad is ready to be published. All you need to do is click the publish button and Facebook will review the ads and confirm it. After some time the ads will be live on facebook newsfeed!

CHAPTER 11. QUORA MARKETING

Quora is a question and answer platform. People ask a direct question about the problem they are facing and request an expert answer to that question.

With Quora, you can generate thousands of targeted traffic to your store in less than few days of using the platform effectively. Don't worry if you are not an expert in that niche.

All you need to do is answer roughly 10 to 15 questions in that niche. Don't forget to say little about yourself in your bio. Make your bio look professional.

You can get a related question by typing your niche into the search box e.g. unicorn

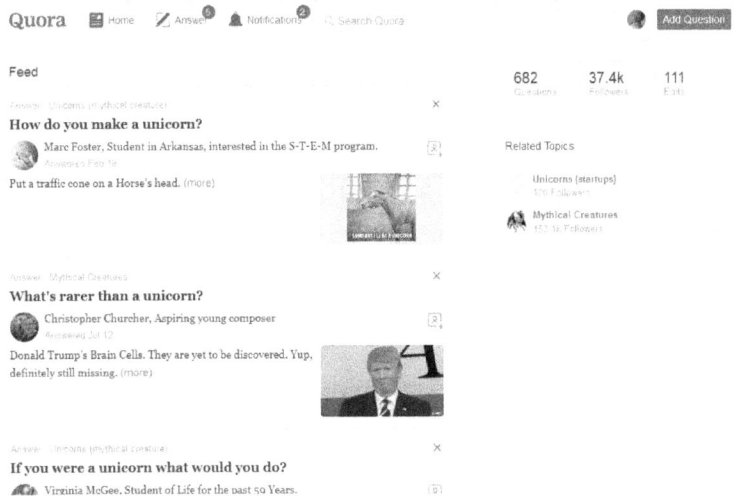

Now you see that there is an unlimited question you can answer under unicorn. Don't worry if you don't know what to say to each question. Since you don't know anything about a unicorn, this is how you can answer the question under the unicorn niche.

- ✓ Goto to busszumo.com
- ✓ Type your keyword in the search box (unicorn)
- ✓ Click on the post that has a good social share
- ✓ Copy few sentence and post on the question you want to post
- ✓ Copy the post URL link and link back to the website from Quora
- ✓ Do this for ten or fifteen different question

You can also use this same step above by typing niche into google.com and follow the step above.

After you have answered up to ten to fifteen question is time for the reward. Is time to link back to your store directly from Quora

- ✓ Copy link from your site URL. Either a blog you post on your store or a specific product you want to promote

- ✓ Search for question or ask a question yourself and answer it, post link as an answer or say some word and link back to your answer

Once you have done the above step the next step is to make our answer to be on top of anyone answer for that question. By doing so we will get a lot and tons of view for our answer which will drive people back to the link we provided.

Follow the step above to get this done

- ✓ Go to boostupvotes.com/buy-quora-upvotes/
- ✓ Buy only 10 upvotes for just $5.99

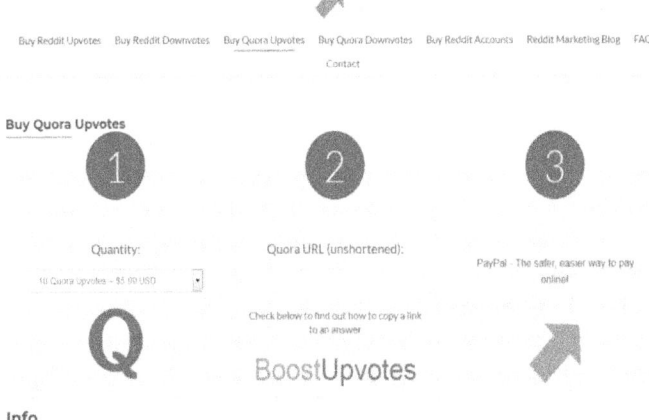

After you have done this you will see your question ranked from other question.

When searching for the question to answer, make sure you use buy term.

Chapter 12. Reddit Marketing

With Reddit, you will be able to get unlimited free targeted traffic like Quora.

To get started subscribe to similar subreddit to your niche. Make sure your read each subreddit post before posting your content this is because Reddit is very strict and subreddit moderators are good at blocking the user.

When you post your content at subreddit. Click the New tab to know if your post is live. If your post is not on the new section that shows that your post is not live on that subreddit but if you found it on the New section that shows that your post is live on that subreddit.

Before you make your first post, make sure to be active in the subreddit related to your niche by commenting on other people post

If you master reddit very well, you can get insane traffic to your store in no matter of times. All you need is to read each subreddit require to avoid being blocked from that subreddit.

About The Author

DAVID NELSON is an Affiliate Marketer, Social Media Marketer, eBay and Shopify Dropshipper, Content Creation and Marketer, Email Marketer, Funnel Builder, SEO and Business Consultant.

After studying the field above for four years, he decided to publish a book on kindle to help people who can't afford hundred and thousand of dollar buy courses online.

David also loves educating and inspiring entrepreneurs to succeed and live the life of their dreams.

Other Books By David Nelson

Keep your eye on the more upcoming book by David Nelson that will make you start a profitable online business and live the lifestyle you deserve while working at your convenient time.

Connect With Me

If you will love to ask me any question, you can do so by following me on instagram.com/davidnelsonofficial/ and quora.com/profile/David-Nelson-399

Connecting with me on this three platform will be a great idea to reach out to me and know when I will be releasing another book that will help you make money online and live the lifestyle you wish for

Leave A Review

If you enjoyed this book or found it useful I'd be very grateful if you'd post a short review on Amazon. Your support really does make a difference and I read all the reviews personally so I can get your feedback and make this book even better.

https://www.amazon.com/dp/B07G2X1NSQ

Thanks again for your support!

www.ingramcontent.com/pod-product-compliance
Lightning Source LLC
Chambersburg PA
CBHW052334220526
45472CB00001B/423